The COVID-19 pandemic sparked a call to nature for many, especially women, and Nancy Austin's new poetry collection *Something Novel Came in Spring* exemplifies this phenomenon. The interiority of the poems is compelling, and the choice of "novel" in the title is not an accident. The poems explore the unseen and unknown. The poet is masked and unmasked. In the poem "Let Ornithology Call the Day," she says, "I'll stop questioning everything," but the poems do the exact opposite. They explicate sunrise and tamaracks, "musing more and missing more." Birdsong is more than noise from the throat of a bird. Birds are a bellwether. Austin writes, "I *have* learned the songbird's names / I *have* learned their many calls." It's this insistence that drives the poems during a time of "desperate search."

Austin explores the intimate and the political, the lessons and loons. In an era of virus, she becomes a new grandmother and worries—genuinely so—about the "children of pandemic." She contends with her own darkness and rallies to "outrace it." Austin's words offer welcome, delight but also deep contemplation where "darkest nights reveal the most stars." In the end, Austin makes an argument for the triumph of humanity, for a "contagion of kindness." Then, she "rests her oars." *Something Novel Came in Spring* is a collection that marks an important crossroad and points forward to signposts of hope.

—Tori Grant Welhouse, author of award-winning *Vaginas Need Air*

If poetry is the language of the soul, how does a poet speak during quarantine? In *Something Novel Came in Spring*, Austin asks if the quarantine splays open our shortcomings, threatens to unravel all that was? Isolation from relationships is a hardship told in a daughter's difficult pregnancy during a heart-wrenching separation as a perfect storm, but the joy of a new grandson is just perfect, or the fatigue of it all told "In the Scream of Things." Yet familiar activities become respites such as birdwatching ("Let Ornithology Call the Day") or star gazing ("COVID Camping"). Even political turmoil of the year is a shared lament, *I—Can't—Breathe* ("Larcenia's Son"). Chapters flow from The Mourning Moon to The Hope Moon, the poet now knowing to be "mindful of the intricacies of the ordinary." Austin's poetry takes the reader on a shared journey.

—Pat Carney, author of *A Kayak is My Church Pew, Bird Brains,* and *To the MU(sic).*

Something Novel Came in Spring

Nancy Austin

SOMETHING NOVEL CAME IN SPRING

Nancy Austin

Water's Edge Press

Copyright © 2021 by Nancy Austin

All rights reserved.

Printed in the United States of America

Water's Edge Press LLC
Sheboygan, WI
watersedgepress.com

ISBN: 978-1-952526-05-3
Library of Congress Control Number: 2021942350

Credits:

Cover image licensed through VectorStock

A WATER'S EDGE PRESS FIRST EDITION

In gratitude to doctors, nurses, and frontline workers who will bear the emotional and physical burdens of all they have endured, long after the pandemic ends. To the families of those who gave their lives or wellbeing.

For my grandsons.

SOMETHING NOVEL

Safe House 1
Something Novel Came in Spring 2
Evan on the Outside 3
As a Pandemic Unfolds, Two Interviews 4
Four Months In 5
Making Soup with Yo-Yo Ma 6
Haiku Trilogy 7
As You Knew I Would 8

MOURNING MOON

YouTube From Italy 11
Songbird-Raptor 12
Funeral Flowers 13
Piano Suite 14
Let Ornithology Call the Day 16
In the Scream of Things 17
Her Last Full Moon 18
Migrations 19
Dreams in the Time of COVID 20

PARALLEL PANDEMIC

America, Unmasked 23
Errrr, Rona 24
CDC is Killing Me 25
Birds Not of a Feather 26
Larcenia's Son 27
COVID Comes in Like a Comet 28
The Logistics of Conspiracy Theories 29
The Sun's Position 30
Early November, 2020 31

YOUR WINGS

Loons Stick an Icy Landing 35
Cabin Fever 36
Creature Comforts 37
COVID Camping 38
Weather's Apostles 39
Apostles Refugium 40
This Still Life 41
A Moment's Embrace 42

MUSE MORE

Who Cooks for You? 45
Lucia and Pietro 46
Lessons of Yearning 47
Lessons from a Cantaloupe 48
Checkout Girl, Aisle Six 49
Since the Gift Giving 50
I Rest My Oars 51
The Pruning 52
Paradigm Shift 53

HOPE MOON

Pioneers of Paper Land 57
Gramma-the-Phone 58
A Return to Ordinary 59
Close to Christmas 60
After Vaccines 62
The River Waits 63
The Year 2020 64
The Pandemic Moon 65

SOMETHING NOVEL

Safe House

I stand in line at Chicago's O'Hare,
immersed in exotic languages, converse

with a couple from India while boarding.
At Denver International, a mystery virus

inundates news as travelers cram
into planes, hip to hip, in rows of ten.

We've been told masks aren't effective,
our country has it under control.

Things accelerate on my trip,
I buy sanitizer, vow not to touch

my mouth or magazines on flights home.
Whispers go viral, words like Ebola

from a nervous woman next to me.
A man sneezes, a woman coughs;

we don't know it's airborne.
I drive hours to get back home

to the secluded Northwoods,
where, for a while, I'll feel safe.

Something Novel Came in Spring

Knee-deep in April Northwoods snow
there was no chickadee's vernal call,
no carefree, lazy, high, low,
seasonal cheer, absent here.

Blackbirds bemoaned a vanquished spring,
drifts smothered daffodils, tree blooms
blackened, robins perished on roadways
in search of worms.

Only the chickadee's sentinel call,
urgent notes to rally the reticent.
Birds of all kind gathered, dove,
drove away a swooping goshawk.

I watched as birds defended their home,
outwitted a well-known enemy.
I scanned the grass, trees, horizon
for my foe—novel, unknown, unseen.

Evan on the Outside

Morning sickness day and night, my daughter
can't keep food down, loses weight.
Medical issues pile up like dirty laundry:
gestational diabetes, low iron, low B-6.
Smooth sailing is surely ahead I tell her,
but her thyroid crashes, her liver enlarges,
ankles so swollen a finger push leaves a pit.

We arrive the eve of delivery, wiggle my mother's
ring onto her once slender pinky for good luck,
kiss her forehead, hug her husband, send them forth.
We cheer news of Evan's arrival, head down the hall
where a nervous nurse catches up, implores us to wait.
A rapid response team hurries into her room.

Her blood pressure soars, liver, kidney labs spike,
platelets plunge, a magnesium drip staves off seizures
at the price of delirium, nausea, muscle contractions.
Her husband places ice packs on her fiery skin,
nurses pump and dump her milk, dried, cracked
lips whisper *Mama, am I ok?*

A week later we huddle in their sun-dappled den,
white walls waiting to be painted seafoam green.
Evan suckles at full breasts, opens his eyes.
We trace his tiny digits, cup his little feet.
He is mellow; he is lovely.
I lean into my daughter's ear to say,
Evan on the inside, a perfect storm.
Evan on the outside—perfect.

As a Pandemic Unfolds, Two Interviews

A celebrity daredevil who lost family to this calling
dons a gasmask, tiptoes across a tightrope over
the Masaya volcano as lava boils below.
Eyes burn, wind blows, smoke obstructs his view.

A celebrity with pancreatic cancer endures
bone-deep bouts of depression, brutal chemo,
tells of his intent to beat slim odds, for his wife,
his love of life, the hope of cancer cohorts.

One spites death, one fights death, I hide from it,
tucked in my easy chair, indebted to those running
towards it: unarmed doctors, nurses, pharmacy techs,
shopkeepers, the kind old man who delivers my groceries.

Four Months In

My daughter and her husband get off work,
quarantine for 14 days, son and grandson as well.
My husband and I shelter alone.
We all drive hours and hours toward each other.

I sanitize, set up the condo kitchen.
My daughter arrives, I bury my head in her
soft hair until she whispers, *Mama, its ok*.
I hug her husband; he unloads the car seat.

Oh, the baby! Not yet into stranger danger,
he reaches up, lays his velvet head on my chest,
smells of sweet melon, is learning to giggle.
He holds my finger, studies my face.

My son's car pulls up, I envelop my grandson
who grew a mustache, whose voice has changed.
My son's curly hair blows in the warm breeze.
He sees his sister, says *Hi Turkey*, with that eye-twinkle.

I make dinner, watching them interact all the while.
Eggplant for my son, rellenos for my grandson,
my daughter's favorite pasta, brownies for her husband.
We retell family stories, hold each other's gaze.

The cuckoo clock startles me, but instead of cuckoo
I hear *trouble, trouble, trouble, trouble*.
Eyes blurred, I drop the gifted *Journal of Dreams*,
stare at walls, wait for the next call, FaceTime, Zoom.

Making Soup with Yo-Yo Ma

I bathe the last of the lentils, slip in
spices as if I can get more, course cut
carrots, eyes moist I chop celery,
onions, air cello between stirs.

Yo-yo plays *The Swan*, I go to the window,
see buds on aspen, morning cloaks, carefree.
Red squirrels chase each other, unaffected.
They don't know.

I shelter in, make soup, keep it to a simmer.
My son calls, tells of his job, a shortage of gloves.
His sister FaceTimes the baby, applied for a leave
to keep them safe. All our kids have essential jobs.

As a girl I dutifully watched *The Wizard of OZ*
each Thanksgiving, hands over eyes helpless
when music cued the fiendish flying monkeys
to swoop over the land.

This menacing music overtakes Yo-yo's calming
concerto as I try not to dwell on Dad stranded
in Arizona at age ninety-five.
The carefully controlled soup boils over.

Haiku Trilogy

spoon in ice cream pail
on dusty monthly planner
—how COVID pounds us

heartless hunter keen
to the doe has filled his tag
but she's deep in snow

a breeze parts the reeds
of an unattended nest
vulture changes course

As You Knew I Would

You scrape your knee, a small cut, but now a boy
who misses his mom, and the men aren't having it.
I drop my book, as any grandma would,
only woman, only sympathizer home.

I scoop you up, as you knew I would,
carry you to the rocker, swaddle you in my arms,
lean in, question softly through sobs
to get at the crux of things, you nod
to give me clues, wail when understood.

We rock this state of understanding, you quiet,
save relapses over male insensitivity.
I teach you to trace a circle around the wounded
knee to self-soothe, you manage a smile,
chat about things you want to do, a nature walk,
tic tack toe game with tape on the carpet, then hear
them hoot in the next room, declare *I love you so Grammy*,
scurry off, back to the business of being a little boy.

Any poet would know to end the poem here,
but this remembrance brings me to tears wondering
how children of this pandemic will fare not knowing
the embrace of grandparents, aunts, uncles and friends.

Mourning Moon

YouTube From Italy

A violin resonates from a hospital rooftop in Cremona,
Italy's epicenter, birthplace of exquisite violins.
It rings out over makeshift treatment tents,
shrill of ambulances, wails of grief, the empty
piazza where twelve streets converge.
Workers behind plastic face shields pause,
adjust, assuage ruts worn into their foreheads,
momentarily released.

We wonder, can we outwit this microscopic foe
that has taken hundreds of thousands already,
preys on the slip of a hand into another, splays open
our shortcomings, threatens to unravel all that was?

That we built a Stradivarius, dreamed a language
all would know—sorrow, beauty, horror, hope
carried heart to hands, generation to generation,
devised a way to send it around the globe
far faster than this virus, is something,
isn't it?

Songbird-Raptor

The farmhouse chair chirped on wooden planks
as she lifted her cup from its saucer, lowered
her head to the crimson contents of elderberry tea.

Outside, a shrike, songbird-raptor, black, white
and grey plumage so handsome on the hedgerow,
scans for prey over the pasture, hooked beak in tandem
with head turn, ebony eyes but a glint on a dark mask.

Beseeched by the whir of the bee, the wren, the sparrow,
his white wings flash over meadow milkweed, then blur
in a hover-hunt, to impale his prize on a thorn.

Funeral Flowers

It was three below zero when she returned from the funeral
to a Fed-Ex bouquet box left on the deck.

Deep red roses with stiff outer petals encircled by calla lilies
rimmed in ice crystals, like fluted margaritas.

She trimmed the frozen stems, peeled the outmost petals,
cropped the lily tops, put aspirin in their water.

Next morning the flowers' exterior edges had darkened,
so, the same surgery and nutrients, then the next day, and the next.

That sundown she gathered the whittled, withered buds in her arms
and let go, when even hope cried out—*enough*.

Piano Suite

I. Piano in the Dark

The shuffle of slippers
down the hall
where kids can't hear,
lit by a reliable moon
full and low
in curtain-less windows
above homes enswathed
in snow,
safe
from chord storms,
minor keys
that crumble
to arpeggios,
a lonely mantra
without words.

II. Prelude to Piano

A low sound,
guttural,
animal,
a moan,
a wail,
someone's wailing.

The phone is broken,
a broken phone,
like it fell,
red spots,
on knees,
on kneecaps,
red spots on kneecaps

Oh God

that sound
is me.

Let Ornithology Call the Day

A phoebe awakens me on Monday.
Phoebe. Phoebe? Phoebe. Phoebe?
I'll stop questioning everything.

An eastern towhee on Tuesday.
Drink your tea, drink your tea.
I'll sip jasmine on the sun porch.

A robin on Wednesday.
Cheer-up cheerily, cheer-up cheerily.
I'll release yesterday's funk.

A hermit thrush on Thursday.
Here I am right near you.
I'll sort the photos in the shoebox.

A crow calls on Friday.
Caw, caw, caw.
I'll call back my friends.

The ovenbird on Saturday.
Teacher-teacher-teacher-teacher.
I'll read Rumi today.

On Sunday, a mourning dove coos
soft as my mother's* sigh.
I'll lay lilacs on her grave.

father, grandma, grandpa, husband, wife, partner, lover, daughter, son, brother, sister, aunt, uncle, nephew, niece, cousin, friend, doctor, nurse, teacher, neighbor, counselor, mailman, babysitter, co-worker, mentor, hairstylist, dentist, veterinarian...

In the Scream of Things

Beds line the halls, code blues beseech, nurses plead
they can't keep pace with surreal shifts, shortages
of staff, surgical masks. Fear of infecting loved ones,
selves, floating faces of deceased disrupt their sleep.

One tells of a co-worker, Mary, off the ventilator,
lucid, so he left to tend others, returned to find her gone.
She died alone. They all die alone, he whispers,
some on Facetime while nurses hold phones.

Down the road Jim clinks his beer mug into Jon's,
weaves through the crowd to get refills.
The bartender, mortgage overdue,
tries not to think of two regulars who died.

College students pour out of campus on holiday,
go home, pack bars, reconnect with friends.
Concerned parents don masks and distance,
deniers, COVID-fatigued gather for Thanksgiving.

Her Last Full Moon

Tonight I learn the last full moon before winter solstice
is called the Mourning Moon. I learn my friend,
adopted mom, former neighbor is dying.
Her son laments the family's struggle to visit her
assisted home during COVID, enjoins friends
to hold vigil from afar.

Betty bridged decades between us with compelling
conversation, always up on the latest books.
When our teen was alone one night, she wore
a stern old lady look and a coat over her nightgown
to expel his raucous partygoers at midnight.

Gifted with good health and endless energy she
visited "shut ins" daily, many younger than herself.
Pudgy after my divorce, she said I had a beautiful
complexion, a way with words, sat on my couch,
listened without interruption, held me as I sobbed,
roles that reversed when Alzheimer's took her husband.

She visited so many in their time of need,
now we celebrate her long, laudable life
as she rises with the Mourning Moon,
last full moon before winter's solstice.

Migrations

You tersely admonished
I refused to retain how to work
the woodstove, instructed at length,
quizzed doggedly the terms.
Not *vowels*, you said, slipping a pill
under your tongue, *volatiles*,
volatile organic compounds.
I owe you my attention, you scolded.
I smiled to myself, saw vowels
i, o, and u, floating up the stove pipe,
tried harder to appease, gently reminded
I *have* learned the songbird's names
I *have* learned their many calls
I *have* learned your woodsman ways.

Today I top loaded the logs,
opened wide the primary air,
engaged the catalytic element
into its secondary combustion,
felt the familiar wave of heat
blanket the cabin and release me.

Only then could I return
to my post at the window.
Stark and cold the leafless birch,
dark the thistle seeds that fell
from the feeder and peppered
the porcelain snow below,
like the black whiskers you left
in the bathroom sink.

Pine grosbeaks picked at the seeds,
looked around, nervous that dusk
would overtake them. But among them
I spotted the curious, lone robin you said
stayed too long into winter's chill,
look up and trill *cheer-up*, *cheerily*,
cheer-up cheerily, as he flew away.

Dreams in the Time of COVID

Unfamiliar city people I wander carrying winter coat laptop squeeze through crowded lobby vendors excuse me excuse pivot sideways can't remember what conference pulled through life by string on forehead many matters to take up if I saw a sign I'd remember concierge points long hall a left a right always lost in the eyes of teller never hear directions on an elevator find myself outdoors car filled avenue sprays slushy snow then warm summer neighborhood sunshine green lawns exotic sounding man under Ford Torino bare legs arms sticking out he says to friend with wrench Rumi saved his life I call from sidewalk I too am steered towards his work he turns a smile his whole naked unabashed openness avert my eyes a friendly wave continue dead end wraparound porch oceanside resort tyrannosaurus rex dallies in shallows animated sign welcome children my one year old son in my arms soft chubby legs propped left hip face pressed corn silk hair scent no tear baby shampoo coos giant orange striped squirrel garden sunflowers big as platters dance whisper his pink ear must be dream you are grown tiny hand my cheek gives earring twirl leans backwards grins woman behind remember as boy cat sitting you crouched down rubbed its neck will be ok your mama coming back dream ending oh stay for walk back he doesn't speak gift his loving nature joy this soul window must find pen paper weep into words.

PARALLEL PANDEMIC

America, Unmasked

Tourists in our town spill out of shops,
pack eateries, cram into lines for ice cream.
No masks, except a woman with a stroller.
Masked, I ask a man for help at Home Depot,
he warns me no one can make him wear one,
it violates his freedom; this virus is a hoax.

Walking into Kwik Trip masked I feel
other's eyes on me as if being mocked,
a man pulls the door shut rather than extend it,
and I wonder if I'm imagining disdain.

Masks, shown to slow the spread, foster contention:
A park ranger pushed in a lake over a mask.
A security guard urging compliance, killed.
An enraged woman coughs in the face of another
who reminds masks there are mandatory,
our highest leaders refrain, even when speaking
with WWII vets.

Most countries mandate compliance,
but we are seduced by individualism,
see masks as political signposts.
COVID has laid open old wounds,
exposed a parallel pandemic with symptoms
of selfishness, racism, misinformation,
a loss of goodwill.
America is unmasked.

Errrr, Rona

My grandson, instructed to back away from a friend,
clenches his fists, purses his lips, stiffens his arms,
yells *Errrrr, Rona*, as he reluctantly complies.
Pressed to wear a mask, he shakes his head,
Errrrr, Rona, through layers of cloth.
Reminded to wash his hands, he utters
Errrrr, Rona, over stomps to the bathroom.

What if, when dreading the mask, hand sanitizer,
six-foot distance, when missing handshakes,
hugs, trips, festivals, beaches, drinks in bars,
when lamenting job loss, lack of intimacy,
what if instead of tossing bipartisan hand grenades,
fixating on misinformation, squandering opportunities
we shift blame to its viral source, stop in our tracks,
clench our fists and holler, *Errrr, Rona*?
Could we then outwit it?

CDC is Killing Me

CDC compromised its legacy,
let politics trump science,
CDC is killing me.

Its guidance doled out carelessly
to court government alliance,
CDC compromised its legacy.

Its stance on masks changed drastically
when unable to supply us,
CDC is killing me.

Botched tests, unproven therapies,
false claims are met with silence,
CDC compromised its legacy.

Watered down advice for schools, for commerce no decrees,
ever changing guidance fosters public noncompliance,
CDC is killing me.

Once revered, its agency leads a COVID-ravaged country,
has it forgotten we the people are its clients?
CDC compromised its legacy,
CDC is killing me.

Birds Not of a Feather

My husband yells *drop everything*, binoculars in hand,
points to a black bird on our birch—grey bib and collar,
a breast rosier than a robin, heavily blushed cheeks.

A different bird, it hops like a woodpecker, forages
like a flycatcher, dazzles with deep wingbeats of a crow,
stays for days, squeaks a language we don't know.

We search bird books in vain, consult computers,
learn of its discovery on Lewis and Clark's journey,
breathlessly tell our neighbors, a *Lewis's Woodpecker*.

We laud this off-course avian, study its habitat, set a place
at our yard's table, host legions of birders who flock from afar,
perch on our treetop balcony to receive this odd bird.

Odd indeed how we open our arms to the foreign bird
yet spurn a woman who walks from Guatemala, parents
who traverse a raging river, their fledglings now caged.

Larcenia's Son

I—Can't—Breathe,
gasps another COVID patient, hand to throat.
A ventilation team rushes in, their faces alert, intent.
A nurse squeezes his hand, explains the procedure,
contacts his family to share quick words on FaceTime.

I—Can't—Breathe,
Oregon residents exclaim as walls of wildfires close in
from all sides, neighbors rush to help neighbors follow
firefighters whose soot covered faces hide trepidation
that all may not be saved.

I—Can't—Breathe,
should compel any mother, father, sister, brother, neighbor,
stranger to rush in with aid, yet when George utters them
face down, hands shackled, neck under the hard-pressed
knee, Adam's apple ground into cold ground, windpipe
constricted, he pleads, summons his mama. The officer's hands,
casually placed in his pants pockets, reflect his stoic expression,
fellow officers block bystanders, George's limbs go limp,
he loses his heartbeat, his breath, his life.

COVID Comes in Like a Comet

A bright green fireball hurls towards earth
at breakneck speed, impact in three days.
Two astrophysicists agree on a fix.
A bill is rushed to the House.

Republicans to the democrat scientist:
We found you had an affair with a woman
whose mechanic once lived in Iran.
Democrats to the republican scientist:
Your accountant is rumored to be Russian.

Investigations are launched.
CNN referees panel discussions.
Fox chronicles meteor conspiracies.
The president touts the growing economy.
A bill is blocked by science deniers.

Leif stacks Legos on the living room rug.
Dhruv star-gazes on a ridge above New Delhi.
Hassan tilts his face towards Mecca.
Brittany twirls at the DMV, first license in hand.
Atsuko serves tea in her Japanese garden.
All blown to space dust, organic material and ice.

The Logistics of Conspiracy Theories

To be an American in 2020 is to live in a petri dish for growing conspiracy theories.
—Zack Stanton, Politico Magazine

Bad dogs
get you to walk them
hand you the leash,
yank you through thistles,
their coats thick as fleece.

Bad dogs
cozy up to your loved ones,
loved ones in need,
sneer, growl and nip you,
when they're not seen.

Bad dogs
make you look callous
if you don't keep pace,
if you don't play ball,
branches scraping your face.

Bad dogs
know your loved ones will follow,
they won't drop the leash,
while they've slyly pulled them
into the street.

The Sun's Position

I walked a winter road weighed down,
not by heavy garments, but by the horrid breath
of hate on news, in editorials, words of a neighbor.

I lumbered such a distance I had to rally to outrace
the dark hours that now outnumbered light,
my earthly impact so slight I could hardly lift my legs.

A melted rivet of water chiseled a hollow in the snowscape.
There, a bit of thaw to arouse the vernal season and remind
that in time, the sun will always break the back of winter.

Early November, 2020

Watching news of plague, superstorms, fire tornados,
peaceful protests usurped by violence, demonizing of science,

I'm sickened, worried evil may have the upper hand,
no matter what we do.

I retreat to the treetop deck. Robust winds swirl branches
of oak and maple, whisk through pines like a brisk broom

clears floors of grime and shriveled scraps.
I repot cuttings from the root-rotted weeping fig,

nubile roots fresh and clean in a glass of clear water.
I bring this promise into my home, return to the deck

to stand with its kin, let wind that lifts their branches
brush through my hair. I raise my arms and am lifted.

YOUR WINGS

Loons Stick an Icy Landing

A tremulous shriek pierces our sleep,
brings us to our feet knowing the bay's
ice cracked open just last night.

Our lake's docile male, 26 years-old,
is monitored by the Loon Project,
most elderly male in their study.

This year, more than ever, we await
our talisman, worried ice-out is late,
as loons land only on water.

But there he is, blood red eyes,
lustrous black head, pinstriped collar,
bobbing, diving through steely grey slush.

Riding low on water, he yodels
for his mate, not seen, to join him.
We exhale when momentarily, she does.

Cabin Fever

His snowshoes crush a path
through thigh-high drifts.
He stops to inspect rabbit tracks,
bits of bone, broken branches.
He doesn't respond when she points to
the periwinkle sky, and snow that stays clean.
He doesn't reply when she asks
if she talks too much.

She sings folksongs out loud because she can up here,
heeds the sun's new position, falls behind to listen
to the last of winter's stillness, and with eyes closed,
can almost feel the rush of spring.
She reaches with a branch to write names
of their children and grandchildren in a smooth
sunny strip of snow, along the trail cut between red pines,
names that will only be seen by the wind that erases them.

On the way back they trace the same path.
He stops to listen to the season's first robin,
and spots both of their names encased in a heart.
He stares a long while, grabs a stick, draws
an arrowhead on one side, fletching on the other,
and in silence turns, continues on.

Creature Comforts

If sheltering alone too long,
go to the woods.
Walk briskly until spent.
Walk more.

There's a low hanging limb
bent like an elbow beneath
a stooping tree.
Nestle in.

Whistle softly,
one high, two lows
for chickadees, sparrows,
their freedom, their joy, your wings.

COVID Camping

As this virus ticks on we try to outwit it,
buy a truck bed tent to join family at a cabin.
We park on a clearing in the woods.

The air mattress inflates like a lifeboat, fills the tent.
Senior status, nothing to hold onto, my brain has no idea
how to launch this tangle of linens from step ladder
to airbed, until my husband pushes my backside.

When one turns over the other is jostled into the air,
seasick until settled in. Soon, our bladders wake us.
No ledge to grab, no floor to place feet, we wrestle the whale,
bump into, knock each other sideways, no forward progress.
I envision a trampoline, rock violently knees to chest,
land close to the target. My husband watches,
shrugs, inchworms his way out.
Knees aching, we climb down into clogs,
follow a flashlight to and from the outhouse.

Invigorated, I lay awake thinking of family, friends,
those whose jobs preclude them from sheltering in.
Barred owls and coyotes call, a breeze sweeps through
screens, the moonless night reveals more constellations
and celestial objects than one could imagine.
Funny how the darkest nights reveal the most stars.

Weather's Apostles

Wind, rain, and waves—fickle potters—reshape
sandstone islands into arches and estuaries,
shape-shift beaches, batter bedrock outcrops
into cliffs, lakeshore rock into sea chambers.

Locals learn to read clouds, visitors, marine
forecasts that can turn a kayak's slip through
placid blue-green waters to peril in sudden squalls,
or in rogue waves that bounce off sea caves.

Errant north winds stymy a good start to winter's
ice bridges overnight, then mellow and mingle
with the lake's warmer water to concoct sea smoke,
copious steam that rolls and rises like a dream.

Apostles Refugium

> ...*when humanity hunkered down, the animal world quickly noted our absence. Some species that had grown dependent on us were left to scramble, while others, emboldened, began reclaiming places...* –Nature is Returning, *Sierra,* National Magazine of Sierra Club

On mainland Wisconsin, when hemlock and white pine reigned,
martens dwelled cat-like in canopies, mole-like in subnivean spaces,
the burrows and runways beneath snow that teemed with shrews and
voles, safe from foxes, fishers, seekers of soft, shiny pelts.

Then forests were logged, closed canopies replaced by birch
and aspen, snowfall dwindled, martens became endangered.
Forty years later, in the archipelago of the Great Lake,
by lake ice, by translocation, slender, silky migrants reappear.

They tumble, play wrestle, propagate, take refuge in the island's
complex canopies, dense understory ripe with red-backed voles.
An almost lost species peers large-eyed from hollow trees,
takes foothold with sharp, curved claws.

This Still Life

The landscape, at the end of the day
is awash with prospect,
like hands poised over a piano.
The water's calm coaxes the sun's rays
to skip like stones on her glassy plane,
a darting dance of diamonds.
With chair pulled close to the canvas
her hands become
the swoop of a swallow,
the bob of each blossom,
the deep wing beat of a heron,
the yearning in tag alders and tamaracks,
the delight of the diaphanous clouds
waiting to uncover the moon.

A Moment's Embrace

The sun's glint
   off a polished paddle

the periphery of the lake
   so familiar

the thick dragonfly buzz
   past the ear

the water's slap
   on the keel

the sun-glow drop
   in the trees

the caress
   of a waning wind

the call
   of the day's last crow

the water
   now indigo ink.

MUSE MORE

Who Cooks for You?

A barred owl lights by my window,
piercing night air with incessant questions.
Months of restless isolation compel me
to answer, *I* do, *I* cook. Yet, he persists.

After much discourse my mentor
of few answers repeats his question,
until I ask, *who, what feeds me*?
He answers in hoots, caws, gaggles.

My thoughts shift from stormy
to bits of blue sky: the slowing
of the clock, alliance with nature,
awareness of things never noticed,

time to reflect, tighter connections,
the privilege of staying home.
I muse on these graces, drift off
to sleep, arms around gratitude.

Lucia and Pietro

These days I muse more, miss the many
facets of my life, even my Sicilian
surname, though Austin is easy.
Mom taught us to help others spell it,
gave us common names *for balance*.
How we sisters loved our cousin's names,
Rita, Rosann, Gera, so we chose secret
Sicilian names, Lucinda, Serafina, Natalia.

Grandparents Lucia and Pietro, long gone,
left labyrinthine cobbled streets, medieval charm
of the Madonie mountains for Ellis Island,
to become Lucy and Peter. Did they choose
their new names? Miss the old?
Invoke them in a crescendo of Italian,
whispered only in the dark?

Lessons of Yearning

As a girl, I longed to live on a lake,
wake to sheer curtains tickling my nose
as a breeze pulled them to and from the screen
to the pulse of waves that swallowed sand.

We lived within blocks of a crystal-clear lake,
fashioned homemade rafts that soared, then sank,
until Dad bought a sailboat and a flaxen fiberglass
canoe we called The Yellow Venture.

I paddled the perimeter, assessed each home's character,
drifted in its dreams to tend that garden, sun on this pier,
swim with those people out to that raft, fold a billowing
sail on their plush, lakeside lawn.

I'd steal back in Yellow Venture before dusk, launch
toward eastern abodes that owned the sunsets,
content to share them in rows of polished plate glass
ablaze in apricot, violet, crimson.

Lessons from a Cantaloupe

Far from a farmer's market or upscale shop,
this discount store melon bore no scent,
no fancy sticker, sure to be tasteless,
this cantaloupe poser.

The interloper puckered a bit while ripening,
prompting an early carve, its flesh firm
against the knife—too firm to be palatable,
a would-be chore to chew.

I plopped pieces into a bowl, served it with cheese
consumed voraciously to assuage hunger, the fault
of this dour fruit I was avoiding. I stabbed a piece,
brought it to my mouth while reading.

Nerves fired, saliva flowed, sweetness startled,
wave upon wave mounted in complexity,
carnal-like utterings escaped through windows,
I dropped my book.

Checkout Girl, Aisle Six

A wisp of hair, streaked blond from Sun In
fell from my ponytail as I adjusted my attitude,
my jean jacket, head down, K-Mart cashier,
high school drop-out, a poem that resists its writing.

A purple-streaked wisp fell from her ponytail
as she adjusted her mask, her jean jacket,
muttered under her trainer's admonitions,
the letters are missing on this keyboard.

A loud woman in line clicked her tongue, railed
Just do it for her, as the checker's face reddened.
She pushed back the purple wisp, steeled herself,
carried on methodically, me up next.

I tried to engage through her rapid eye blinks,
then left, unable to convey her grace, gumption,
and patience could take her anywhere.
If I see her again, I'll slip her this poem.

Since the Gift Giving

The peace lily, years old, is stunted,
all leaves, no blooms since its gifting.
I busy in, out and around this still life,
grateful it survives with little care.

Throw that thing out, my husband advises,

and I take notice of its dormancy,
of my stagnancy since sheltering,
of all I've taken for granted, neglected
to repot, fertilize, coax into bloom.

I Rest My Oars

Hurrying at dawn, I stop on the deck, fish for keys,
hear wolves howl, perhaps as far away
as the raspberry patch down the sand road.

At noon I pour a quick bucket of water on a wilted
hydrangea, too busy to fill the watering can.
Leaves rustle, a perplexed toad pops out.

Mid-day I power through my kayak run.
Hypnotized by the sun's warmth, I rest my oars,
wake to a blue heron as still as my beached boat.

In evening I close my computer, slip outside to swoon
over May's Flower Moon, Corn Moon, Milk Moon,
as she lights the deck and trees in soft sepia.

The Pruning

The houseplant, a fig tree, grew lopsided, spindly,
pale limbs lethargic over its gifted Grecian urn.
Pruning, she moved to the window side where it
it flourished, deep green, ambiently nourished.

Stripped of the unruly, the streamlined branches
bled thick and milky, then sealed themselves
from what was lost to send shoots in all directions.
A cutting was left levitating in mid-air.

The overcluttered fig tree, stressed for space,
sent a tendril to traverse the expanse between
inside screen and outside glass, filled it with fine
fig greenery, its sentinel shoot severed, suspended.

She potted the shoot, silenced her cell, closed her laptop,
slipped out the screen door, climbed in her kayak,
wind-milled away from worldly into the world,
lighter, pared, buoyant, bared, levitating in mid-air.

Paradigm Shift

I look back when Dad, in his late 60's, seemed so old.
My sister had to move off campus; our family helped out.
Word spread between us not to let Dad lift the heavy stuff.
I'll never forget, nor did I fully understand, the raw surprise,
hurt and indignation on his face as he caught on.

Until now.

As I winter-prep my garden, I gaze up, see my 66-year-old husband,
his pal, 79, hoist sections of dock onto the lawn,
heave its metal frame stuck in lake muck onto the shoreline,
high five each other. I smile, lift a hefty barrel of garden debris
toward the woods, imagine my own father, now 96, ease down
his front stoop, take in autumn's clear, fresh sky, pause,
then power toward his mailbox.

HOPE MOON

Pioneers of Paper Land

They head to their cabin to shelter in,
round the corner as they had for decades,
find a wasteland of stumps, scraggly brush
where the old growth giants once were,
witness a beast of the forest hover,
hug a tree, weep hydraulic fluid,
delimb branches in one sweep
as easily as a chef strips kale leaves
from its stalk.

After the devastation, the damaged forest floor
sprouts pioneers. Jack pine, aspen, yellow poplar,
paper birch take root in sandy soils, adaptable,
short-lived stand-ins for the lost primeval trees.
Together they colonize, establish canopies,
call back the forest.

Gramma-the-Phone

My ten-month-old grandson, a thousand miles
away, hasn't seen us in seven months.

He peers into the FaceTime screen,
smiles at *it's Gramma-the-phone.*

We wonder what he thinks, never knowing
company in his home, or what a phone is.

Whether he's bouncing or pulling himself up
he stops in his tracks when I whistle,

a sound he's never heard before.
He listens, then resumes his play.

This is how he'll know me.

I envision our reunion over and over.
A stranger, he'll eye me with curiosity,

hold tight to my daughter, look to his Dad
for a cue. I'll sit on the floor, whistle a tune,

announce it's *Gramma-the-phone.*
He'll brighten, grin, scoot into my arms.

A Return to Ordinary

FDA approves first COVID-19 vaccine for emergency use in U.S.
—*NY Times, 11/11/20*

Someday soon, I'll set my stride to my grandson's
two-year old legs, his hand wrapped around my pinky.
He'll shrug his shoulders, blurt non-sensicals with flourishes
of his free arm, meet my eyes with a knowing nod.
A giggle will shake his diminutive frame, as a fat-cheeked
chipmunk peeks out from the crevices of a wood pile.
He'll stoop to finger the shingles on an acorn's bumpy
beret, arch his eyebrows, purse his lips into an O.
I'll teach him to say acorn, together we'll be mindful
of the intricacies of the ordinary.

Close to Christmas

Oh, how they pound,
Raising their sound,
O'er hill and dale,
Telling their tale. —Carol of the Bells

A couple flags us down on the gravel road.
Their dog bolted off when hunters fired shots
nearby, six hours prior. Buddy, a tiny teddy,
afraid of the dark, never leaves their side.
How to tell their kids? We offer hope,
wilderness and weather notwithstanding.

The next day a neighbor brings flyers,
reports the husband spent all night in the woods.
Strangers search, exchange Messenger updates,
bolster one another with pet survival stories.

We drive around, stop here and there, call out,
fantasize him bounding from woods to car,
a joyous reunion, the owner's incredulous looks.
Social media advice abounds, finally a sighting.
A similar breed, lost for hours is found, returned.

Another night, colder yet. Coyotes yip-howl.
Buddy shivering in the wild depresses us
beyond the usual COVID isolation. I project
my loss that lately I can't seem to rise above
onto this desperate search, invest deeper,
wake anxious, lonely. Can a tiny dog survive
predation, another ten-degree night?
Gloomy skies persist, I resume gift wrapping,
my phone lights up, dances and dings repeatedly,
like Carol of the Bells. *Buddy's been found,*
he's been found, I yell down the stairs,
call his owner, learn a man on route to his cabin
spotted Buddy trotting down Camp Nine Road.

The owner and I exchange info like old friends.
She sends pictures of Buddy, wonders why so many
rallied over a stranger's dog in a world of breaking
news, mass casualties, division.

Perhaps a contagion of kindness, or urgency
to sway the outcome of a now familiar tale—
a protagonist, propelled into predatory new lands,
overcomes obstacles, reunites with family and friends.

After Vaccines

I'll break my cellphone addiction,
shave my legs, spill my guts to my hairstylist
as inches fall to the floor, wear lipstick
instead of a mask, relearn to smile.

After vaccines, I'll happy hour around the lake,
hitch everyone's pontoon boat into a floating isle,
airborne laughter droplets rising like cumulus clouds,
unnoticed.

After vaccines, I'll monopoly with grandsons for hours
in a rental condo while our kids cannonball in its pool,
sob when I see my sisters, sip from my brother's glass,
sit close enough to quip with Dad.

After vaccines, I'll squeeze my frail neighbor's hand,
browse in the shops for non-essentials.
Exhausted, at day's end, I'll tumble into bed,
snore through the night, a rescue human freed

from shelter, complete with shots, study subject
in a sequel to Harlow's monkey experiments
reconfirming the ill effects of isolating
primates in their cages.

The River Waits

I dipped my toe in its inky spring
at seventeen, waded, left too soon.

Decades drummed, words hummed
like tinnitus beneath pagers, cell phones,

college books, exams, soured milk,
soiled diapers, a desk piled high.

Now my desk is a riverbank willow where
I heed the rustle of alders, shouts of birch,

murmurs of elders, and all whose narratives
burble in the shallows, shoot the rapids.

I toss petals into the current to whirly-gig
in endless eddies, to sail this river of words.

The Year 2020

On this day, a trifecta unfolds.
A new moon rises, vaccines begin,
electoral votes are counted.

On this day we cross the threshold
of three hundred thousand gone,
ascend a steep diagonal line.

On this day, the long ending begins.
Questions that rise from the calendar's
eyes will baffle historians for years.

The Pandemic Moon

Poets wax on about the moon, my delight wanes.
I was taken by its various hues when full:
pink moon, harvest moon, flower moon
that emerged from pines to unfurl its moon-wake
on water. I've fawned over crescent moons hung
haphazard from a star, lauded moon beams
that slipped over my sill to lull me to sleep.

But that was when sons, daughter, and their spouses
hugged me tightly, when I walked with my sisters,
elbows locked, when my brother hosted family BBQ's,
when I could gently embrace my 96-year old Dad.

That was when my grandsons could scramble
onto my lap with a book, giggle into their pjs
when I sang the jammie-up song, when feet,
spent from baseball were propped on my sofa,
when the oldest ones conversed candidly about
their jobs or finding a new girlfriend.
The newest has learned to crawl on Facetime.

Now I see the moon for what it is,
a hunk of airless iron formed from debris,
boiling by day, sub-zero by night,
glass-like lunar soil that reeks
of gunpowder, an empty, distant
vacuum bombarded by comets.

My family looks to me for hope,
but today it is as distant as the moon.
Give me this day to be dark.
Tonight, I will open my blinds,
embrace the hope moon as it rises.

Acknowledgements

A kind thank you to the editors of the following journals or anthologies for publishing these, or earlier versions of the following poems:

A is for Apostle Islands: "Weather's Apostles"

I Can't Breathe: A Poetic Anthology of Fresh Air: "Larcenia's Son"

Gyroscope Review, Kelsay Books (2019): "Let Ornithology Call the Day"

Isolation Zine: "Making Soup with Yo-Yo Ma"

Kosmos Magazine: "Birds Not of a Feather"

Lakeland Times: "Errrr, Rona"

Lockdown 2020: "As the Pandemic Unfolds, Two Interviews" and "You Tube from Italy"

Musings During a Time of Pandemic: A World Anthology on COVID-19: "Four Months In"

RavensPerch: "Pandemic Moon," "Four Months In," and "As You Knew I Would"

Remnants of Warmth (Kelsay Books 2016): "The Still Life," "Migrations," "Cabin Fever," and "Songbird-Raptor"

Sheltering With Poems: Community and Connection During COVID: "America Unmasked" and "Something Novel Comes in Spring"

Island Intersections: Art/Poetry/Science Symposium: "Apostles Refugium"

The Turn of the Tiller, The Spill of the Wind, (Kelsay Books, 2019): "The Sun's Position" and "The Pruning"

About the Author

Nancy Austin relishes time to write in the Northwoods of Wisconsin, land of abundant lakes, scent of pine, call of loons. She holds a master's in psychology and ran a Community Support Program for individuals with mental illness in Green Bay, WI. for many years. Her world centers around family. She has five grandsons and is shooting for a whole baseball team.

Nancy enjoys the connectiveness of both poetry and music to other narratives. Published in various journals such as *Midwest Gothic, Portage Magazine*, and *Gyroscope Review*, her collections include *Remnants of Warmth* (Kelsay Books, 2016), *The Turn of the Tiller, The Spill of the Wind* (Kelsay Books, 2019), and a collaborative anthology with the PaperBirch Poets, called *Stitching Earth to Sky* (Water's Edge Press, 2019).

---

nancyaustinauthor.com

www.ingramcontent.com/pod-product-compliance
Lightning Source LLC
Chambersburg PA
CBHW052120110526
44592CB00013B/1687